D0793758

A BLUE BANNER
BIOGRAPHY

Gwen Stefani

Kathleen Tracy

Mitchell Lane
PUBLISHERS

P.O. Box 196
Hockessin, Delaware 19707
Visit us on the web: www.mitchelllane.com
Comments? email us: mitchelllane@mitchelllane.com

Mitchell Lane PUBLISHERS

Printing		3	4	5	6	7	8	9

Blue Banner Biographies

Akon	Alan Jackson	Alicia Keys
Allen Iverson	Ashanti	Ashlee Simpson
Ashton Kutcher	Avril Lavigne	Bernie Mac
Beyoncé	Bow Wow	Britney Spears
Carrie Underwood	Chris Brown	Chris Daughtry
Christina Aguilera	Christopher Paul Curtis	Ciara
Clay Aiken	Condoleezza Rice	Daniel Radcliffe
David Ortiz	Derek Jeter	Eminem
Eve	Fergie (Stacy Ferguson)	50 Cent
Gwen Stefani	Ice Cube	Jamie Foxx
Ja Rule	Jay-Z	Jennifer Lopez
Jessica Simpson	J. K. Rowling	Johnny Depp
JoJo	Justin Berfield	Justin Timberlake
Kate Hudson	Keith Urban	Kelly Clarkson
Kenny Chesney	Lance Armstrong	Lindsay Lohan
Mariah Carey	Mario	Mary J. Blige
Mary-Kate and Ashley Olsen	Michael Jackson	Miguel Tejada
Missy Elliott	Nancy Pelosi	Nelly
Orlando Bloom	P. Diddy	Paris Hilton
Peyton Manning	Queen Latifah	Ron Howard
Rudy Giuliani	Sally Field	Selena
Shakira	Shirley Temple	Tim McGraw
Usher	Zac Efron	

Library of Congress Cataloging-in-Publication Data
Tracy, Kathleen.
    Gwen Stefani/ by Kathleen Tracy.
        p. cm. -- (Blue banner biographies)
    Includes bibliographical references (p.), discography (p.), and index.
    ISBN 1-58415-514-0 (library bound: alk. paper)   3755 1370 5/09
    1. Stefani, Gwen, 1969- 2. Rock musicians—United States—Biography—Juvenile literature.
    I. Title. II. Series: Blue banner biography.
    ML3930.S74T73 2007
    782. 42164092—dc22
        [B]   2006014802
ISBN-13: 9781584155140

ABOUT THE AUTHOR: Kathleen Tracy has been a journalist for over twenty years. Her writing had been featured in magazines including *The Toronto Star*'s "Star Week," *A&E Biography* magazine, *KidScreen,* and *Variety.* She is also the author of numerous biographies, including *Carrie Underwood, Kelly Clarkson,* and *Mariah Carey* for Mitchell Lane Publishers.

PHOTO CREDITS: Cover: Steve Granitz/WireImage.com; p. 4 Kevin Mazur/WireImage.com; p. 7 Getty Images; p. 11 Kevin Mazur/WireImage.com; p. 13 Steve Granitz/WireImage.com; p. 16 Kevin Mazur/WireImage.com; p. 18 Jim Smeal/WireImage.com; p. 21 Steve Granitz/WireImage.com; p. 24 Kevin Mazur/WireImage.com; p. 29 Steve Granitz/WireImage.com

PUBLISHER'S NOTE: The following story has been thoroughly researched, and to the best of our knowledge represents a true story. While every possible effort has been made to ensure accuracy, the publisher will not assume liability for damages caused by inaccuracies in the data, and makes no warranty on the accuracy of the information contained herein. This story has not been authorized or endorsed by Gwen Stefani.

CONTENTS

Gwen Stefani performs with No Doubt at Mardi Gras in 2002 as part of MTV coverage of the annual event. For over a decade, the band toured relentlessly, playing venues from huge arenas to local festivals. Their years on the road helped No Doubt build an intensely loyal following.

Overcoming Tragedy

*I*t was going to be the most important night of their lives. Just over a year after playing at their first party, a little-known garage band named No Doubt had been booked to play at the infamous Roxy on the Sunset Strip. The band had burst on the underground music scene and quickly gained an avid following because of their high-energy show. What started as a lark had become a possible career for the group of high school friends.

Much of that energy came from front man and cofounder John Spence. He and Eric Stefani, a songwriter and keyboard player, became friends while working together at a local Anaheim, California, Dairy Queen. Later, they would both attend Loara High School. They formed the band after discovering a shared love of ska, which is a cross between island reggae and punk. They recruited Eric's younger sister Gwen to sing backup vocals, and assembled five other musicians, including horn players.

From the beginning, the driving force behind the band was Spence. Ambitious and charismatic, Spence loved performing and pushed the group to be more than just another garage band. At first they called the band Apple Core, but it eventually morphed into No Doubt—which was a phrase Spence used constantly.

In early 1987, the band performed their first professional gig at Fender's in Long Beach, California. They were one of 14 acts on the bill. In the audience that night was guitar player Tony Kanal, who was taken by the band's sound and joined a few weeks later. Tony assumed the duties of manager, as well as helping develop the unique sound No Doubt would become famous for.

Their shows were initially as popular for Spence's antics on stage as for their music. He screamed more than he sang and strutted across stage wearing a hat he called his *fuzzy furry*, which one observer described as looking like a bicycle seat cover that had been ripped open. Then he would thrill the crowd with his signature backflips.

Word soon got around, and No Doubt was invited to perform at the Roxy. Since the 1960s, the Sunset Strip had been home to legendary music clubs where bands such as The Doors got their start. Filled with inventive billboards, neon lights, and cruising cars, the Strip practically vibrates with energy. Over the decades, punk, new wave, glam,

> *In early 1987, the band performed their first professional gig at Fender's in Long Beach, California.*

grunge, and hard rock bands have flocked to the Strip, hoping to get their big break. Although West Hollywood is decidedly more upscale today than in the past, clubs like The Whisky, Key Club, the Viper Room, and the Roxy are still where underground bands go to be seen and heard.

The members of No Doubt knew the Roxy would be filled not just with fans but also with many record label representatives, who were always on the lookout for a new sound. To prepare, John had the band practicing nearly every day, pushing everyone to their limits—including his own.

On December 21, 1987, just days before the most important performance they had ever given, John Spence

No Doubt—Tony Kanal, Gwen Stefani, Adrian Young, and Tom Dumont— underwent several personnel changes in the early years. The band lost both cofounders: John Spence committed suicide shortly before the band was scheduled to perform on the infamous Sunset Strip, and Eric Stefani left over creative differences to pursue a career as an animator.

wrote a two-page letter. Then he took a gun, went to a local park, and killed himself. He was just 18 years old.

For those left behind, suicide never makes sense. But in this case especially, it seemed unfathomable. "None of us were prepared for that, none of us could see that coming," Tony says on the No Doubt web site. "It just kinda happened, it just changed everything."

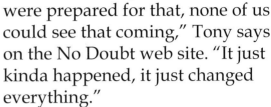

Eric, Gwen, and Tony realized that the best way to remember and honor their friend was to keep the band alive.

Gwen adds, "When your friend dies like that and it's so unexpected it's very traumatic. I think it taught us all a big lesson in how much one person can influence so many different people."

In retrospect, John's antics may have been just a cover for soul-deep unhappiness. Years later, Eric would tell VH-1, "I wish I could have done something." He believes that John might not have been able to handle the pressure of performing at the Roxy, or the pressure of what was at stake.

Although the shell-shocked band performed, they announced it would be their last performance. They could not envision carrying on without John. Then, after a few months' reflection, Eric, Gwen, and Tony realized that the best way to remember and honor their friend was to keep the band alive. Together they would turn tragedy to triumph—and in the process, Gwen would become one of music's biggest stars and most influential songwriters.

Growing Up in the O.C.

*T*he real star of the TV series *The O.C.* was the gorgeous Pacific Coast in California's Orange County, where million-dollar houses perch on rocky cliffs that overlook the ocean. A little inland, the O.C. takes on a less glamorous, more distinctly middle-class sensibility, such as the neighborhood where high school sweethearts Dennis Stefani and Patti Flynn settled after getting married.

Although they were both musicians, and for a while performed on the folk circuit in a group called the Innertubes, they decided against pursuing musical careers. Dennis became a marketing executive and Patti quit her job as a dental assistant after their first child, Eric, was born.

Gwendolyn Renée Stefani was born in Fullerton at St. Jude's Hospital on October 3, 1969. Her sister, Jill, was born three years later, and Todd, the baby of the family, was born in 1974. They grew up in Anaheim, literally in the shadow of Disneyland.

"My mom and dad met at Anaheim High School," Gwen told *The Observer* newspaper. "After they got married, all they wanted to do was have four children— and they did."

They passed along their love of music to their children, often dragging the youngsters with them to festivals and concerts. One of the first performers Gwen remembers seeing was Emmylou Harris. "She had just had a baby and she took a break in the middle of the show to go feed the baby. I couldn't believe it."

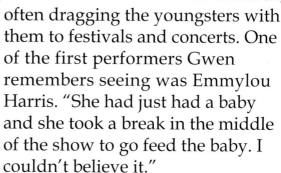

Gwen and Jill would play Musical House, where instead of speaking in sentences they had to sing the words.

Even so, Gwen was inspired enough to put on puppet shows for the neighbors with Eric. She and Jill would play Musical House, where instead of speaking in sentences they had to sing the words. Sometimes Eric would get her to perform with him. One of the first songs he ever wrote was about a pencil sharpener that he called "Stick It in the Hole."

"He was always pounding on the piano and forcing me to come into the living room and sing with him and stuff like that," Gwen said in *Circus* magazine. "He was the one who got me into this. He's my biggest musical influence."

Gwen also readily admits she idolized her older brother. "Everything Eric was into, I got into," she told *The Observer*. "He's super-creative, and he was this high-school cartoonist and had all these wild artist friends.

I don't know if he really was cool or not, but he seemed cool to me."

On the other hand, she describes herself as being lazy and passive. "Growing up, my brother was the one with all the talent and all the focus," Gwen recalled in a *Rolling Stone* interview. "I had him, so I didn't have to do anything, you know?"

As a young teenager, Gwen played piccolo in the marching band and joined the swim team when she attended Loara High School—earning her the nickname Frog. Suffering from a lack of self-confidence, she often struggled in school. She particularly disliked math and worried she might not have good enough grades to graduate.

Stefani's parents, Dennis and Patti, were high school sweethearts. Before settling down to raise a family, they worked as musicians. They passed their love of music to their children and encouraged Gwen to pursue her dream of being a professional performer.

Gwen grew up Catholic and says her parents kept a close eye on their kids. "My mother and father had a really tight leash on me," she said in a Scotland.com interview. At the same time, she adds, "There's lots of great qualities I think they've given me, a lot of great morals. Also, my mom inspired me to be a designer and make clothes, because she's passionate about sewing. And my dad inspired me to do music because he's really creative and always doing music himself."

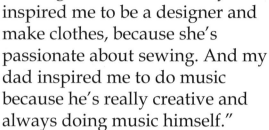

Eric developed an interest in British ska bands such as Madness and The Selecter, so Gwen followed suit.

For a long time, Gwen's musical tastes were on the conservative side—an early idol was Julie Andrews, and two of her favorite albums were the sound tracks from *Annie* and *The Sound of Music*. But then Eric developed an interest in British ska bands such as Madness and The Selecter, so, of course, Gwen followed suit.

Always the instigator, Eric talked Gwen into participating in a school talent show. Wearing a tweed dress her mother had made— identical to a dress Julie Andrews wears in *The Sound of Music*—she got up on stage and sang The Selecter's "On My Radio." After her performance, it came as no surprise when Eric asked Gwen to be the backup singer for the new band he and his close friend John Spence had formed.

At their first public performance—a birthday party in December 1986—Gwen felt at a complete loss on stage. "At that time I was like, *How do I move up here?* Me in my

Stefani goes for a glamorous look at the 2005 Grammy Awards in Los Angeles. Ironically, as a young teenager, Gwen's taste in clothes was relatively conservative. Her mom taught her to sew, and when she was in high school, Gwen often made her own clothes. For a talent show, she wore a replica of the simple smock worn by Julie Andrews in The Sound of Music.

dress," while John dazzled the audience with backflips. But Gwen soon found her footing—and a new fashion sense. "I was super-ska girl," she says. "I wore only black and white and hoop earrings."

When Tony Kanal joined No Doubt in early 1987, the dynamics of the band would be changed forever. Not only was he a talented bass guitarist, but Gwen fell in love and believed he was the boy she was destined to marry.

Early Struggles

*T*ony Kanal had moved to Anaheim from England in 1981, when he was eleven. His parents were Indian, so that made him doubly exotic and fascinating to Gwen. He had been with the band for only a couple of months when she made her move. Stefani told writer Chris Heath that during the summer of 1987, after No Doubt had played at a party one night, she took Tony for a walk and kissed him.

"He thought it was a one-night kiss," she said, "but I was in love."

And soon, so was Kanal — but they were afraid to let anybody else know. "Oh, boy," Tony recalled in *Rolling Stone*. "It was a secret of immense proportions."

Even so, their band mates began to suspect something was going on between them. That Halloween, several of the guys cornered Tony with the threat: "If we find out you're going out with Gwen, you're dead."

Tony denied it, but the stress on both him and Gwen was tremendous. It was only after John Spence's suicide that December that they realized life really can be too short to live a lie. Tony and Gwen announced they were dating and in love and, just like that, everyone else got over it.

In the months after Spence's death, No Doubt slowly reinvented itself. Originally, trumpet player Alan Meade stepped forward and took over lead vocals, but he left the band a short time later—after his girlfriend became pregnant. Almost by default, and on Eric's suggestion, Gwen became lead singer.

"I had no idea I could even sing," she said in *The Independent Sunday* newspaper, "but my brother has always been my leader, and so I just went with it." She juggled her new duties with her studies and part-time job at the local Dairy Queen.

"The managers would leave and we'd all eat," Stefani told the *Washington Post*. "I got so fat when I worked there. And the benches had wood slabs, and these bars. I had to scrub them with a toothbrush to get the fudge off."

The following year, in 1989, guitarist Tom Dumont and drummer Adrian Young joined the band, replacing two other original members who had left. With the addition of Dumont and Young, No Doubt's sound finally gelled.

> "I had no idea I could even sing," Gwen said, "but my brother has always been my leader, and so I just went with it."

After graduating from Loara High School in 1987, Gwen enrolled at Cal State Fullerton, but her primary focus was the band—with her fashion style a close second.

"Ever since I hit puberty, I've been really into having my own look," she told *Cosmopolitan*. "I would buy old

Gwen struts her stuff wearing balance-defying platform shoes at the 2004 MTV European Music Video Awards Show in Rome, Italy. As Stefani became more comfortable being No Doubt's lead singer, she began developing her unique—and often outrageous—fashion sense.

men's pajama bottoms and peg them and wear my monkey boots and my tank tops. I was also really into Hollywood glamour: skinny eyebrows, lots of powder with red-black lips and tons of mascara."

In 1991 Interscope offered the band a record deal. Their debut album, *No Doubt,* sold 30,000 copies, which by music industry standards was a flop. Part of the problem was timing. At that time, grunge music was peaking, with bands like Nirvana and Pearl Jam leading the way with dark, brooding songs. No Doubt's catchy melodies and lyrics seemed jarringly passé, and Gwen's quirky persona turned off the fans who were more into hard rock.

Undaunted, No Doubt hit the road in the fall of 1992 for a two-and-a-half-month tour. In March 1993, Gwen and the others began recording their second album, which would be titled *Tragic Kingdom.* It would take over two and a half years to complete. As they worked on the album, Gwen and her brother Eric began to grow apart.

> *In 1991 Interscope offered the band a record deal. Their debut album, No Doubt, sold 30,000 copies.*

Although he wouldn't admit it until later, Eric felt threatened. First, Interscope strongly urged the band to work with other producers, which angered Eric. But the bigger problem was that as she got older, Gwen began to assert herself. She didn't always just automatically agree with everything her brother said anymore.

Gwen was also starting to discover her songwriting talents—it was she and Tom who wrote the song "Just a Girl," which would become No Doubt's first national hit record. Even though Eric was happy for Gwen, he was still envious.

In 1994, Eric quit the band altogether and took a full-time job animating for *The Simpsons*. As shocking as it was for the band, the rift with her brother was devastating for Gwen. At their parents' urging, she and Eric would go to

Eric and Gwen clown around for photographers at the End of the Tour Party for the Rolling Stones in Las Vegas in February 1998. As kids, Gwen says she idolized her brother. But after Eric left the band in 1994, he was resentful of Gwen, and the siblings had to go through counseling to repair their relationship.

therapy together, which helped repair their relationship. "I didn't want to lose my brother," she told Chris Heath, "because everything that I am is because of him."

That same year, Gwen suffered a second loss when Tony Kanal broke off their seven-year relationship. "I had been ready to get married so it was really hard—he was just totally the love of my life," she says on the site NoDoubtweb.com. He offered to leave the band, but, despite her upset, Gwen wouldn't let him. Somehow, she would figure out a way to cope. One way was to start writing her feelings down as songs.

Stefani said in *Cosmopolitan* that they were able to remain friends because they shared such a "passion for music. We just loved the band so much, and I guess we knew that it was worth it.

"But him breaking up with me was the most incredible thing because before that, I was a very passive person who was dependent on him for my happiness. I was only 17 when I started seeing him, and I never had any other serious boyfriends before that, so I glamorized the relationship and I was so in love.

"When he broke up with me, I started writing all these songs, and I found my talent, which was the most empowering thing that ever happened to me."

It would also make her music's new pop queen.

> **That same year, Gwen suffered a second loss when Tony Kanal broke off their seven-year relationship.**

CHAPTER 4

Tragic Kingdom Magic

*F*inally, in October 1995, *Tragic Kingdom* was released. Initially sales were sluggish, but as "Just a Girl" began to get radio airplay, the album began to take off. Gwen said in *Circus* magazine that she got the idea for the song because of her dad, who "used to yell at me for going to Tony's house and coming home real late. I don't think a lot of guys know what a burden it is to be a girl sometimes."

That fall, No Doubt went back out on tour, opening for Bush. The band's lead singer, Gavin Rossdale, was quickly smitten with Gwen—although initially she wasn't interested. He persisted and eventually they began dating in December 1996. This time being in love proved more complicated for Gwen, because she and Gavin spent so much time apart touring with their respective bands. Again, she would put all that emotion into her songwriting.

By August 1996, *Tragic Kingdom* was certified platinum, which means it had sold a million copies. After ten years of performing, No Doubt was finally a qualified success.

As the band's music became more popular, more and more attention focused on Gwen. And after the release of "Don't Speak" in late 1996—an emotional ballad Gwen

By the time they appeared together at the 2001 MTV Movie Awards in Los Angeles, Gwen and Gavin Rossdale, lead singer for Bush, had been dating for five years. The couple met when No Doubt opened for Bush in 1996.

wrote that was inspired by her breakup with Tony—No Doubt was suddenly overshadowed by people's interest in Gwen Stefani, something the other band members worked hard not to resent.

"At this point, it's something that the rest of us have accepted," Kanal said in a June 1997 *Washington Post* interview, "whereas when it first happened, the impact was pretty awful. We kind of expected it—the lead singer always gets a lot of attention and a female always gets a lot of attention—but we didn't expect it to be as intense as it was."

Magazines began publishing covers featuring only Gwen, and style magazines began following her every move.

Magazines began publishing covers featuring only Gwen, and style magazines began following her every clothes and hair change. By December 1997, fourteen months after its release, *Tragic Kingdom* reached number 1 on Billboard's album list. It would stay there for nine weeks. In all, the album would sell over 10 million copies in the United States alone. It made Gwen a star, especially among teen girls.

"It's amazing to have a connection with girls all over the world that you've never met," Stefani admitted in the *Chicago Tribune.* "No matter where they are in the world, we've shared a lot of the same experiences, have a lot of the same interests. It's great for me to be able to relate."

On New Year's Day, 2002, Gavin proposed to Gwen, and they were married that September. Gwen told *Tragic*

Kingdom fanzine that even though she had always wanted to get married, once the band became successful, she wondered if it would ever happen.

"I always dreamed about it when I was younger but when I got into the reality of life I just didn't see how it was ever going to work out. You have to be so selfish when you're in a band and you're an artist."

But because Rossdale is also in a band and understands the life, they've managed to make their marriage work. "We really got it down; it's really fun for us. Everyone is different but for us it's very romantic, it feels very settled. It's comforting and we're loving it."

In 2003, Gwen was given the chance to make another dream come true when she started her own fashion line. "My stylist, Andrea, and I were making so many outfits that we decided, Why don't we do a clothing line together? It's every girl's dream," she told writer Jennifer Furmaniak. "We were going to do something really small and just sell our stuff at a few boutiques."

Gwen was given the chance to make another dream come true when she started her own fashion line.

As soon as word got out, Stefani was approached by an investor willing to let her keep creative control. She chose the name LAMB for her line in honor of an old pet.

"I had a dog for 16 years, and I called her Lamb because she was like the lamb in 'Mary Had a Little Lamb'—she followed me everywhere I went," Stefani

Gwen hangs out backstage at the LAMB fashion show during Olympus Fashion Week in September 2005. She admits that developing a fashion line is as time-consuming and creatively taxing as songwriting.

explained in *Cosmopolitan*. It was after her first line of bags for LeSportsac came out that she decided, "L should stand for Love, A for Angel, M for Music, and B for Baby."

Her full clothing line debuted in the spring of 2004. Although Gwen told Brandon Griggs that developing the line was "super fun," she also adds, "I don't know what I was thinking. It is so much work, it's exactly like writing a song—it takes a lot of time and effort."

After 17 years of nonstop work, Gwen realized it was time to finally slow down and figure out what she wanted to do with the rest of her life.

Having It All

A fter almost two decades of nearly constant togetherness, and after the release of *Rock Steady*, the members of No Doubt decided to take a vacation from the band and each other. Stefani, now living in London with Rossdale, stressed to *Cosmopolitan* that they were not disbanding but simply recharging "to pursue independent projects."

For Gwen, that was her first solo album, which she titled *Love, Angel, Music, Baby.* She admitted in a June 2004 *Cosmopolitan* interview that it was taking her a while to complete the album.

"It's been hard to focus. Coming off the tour and having my first year of being married, I'm kind of lazy. I like to lie around with my husband and watch TV and stuff like that. It takes a lot of selfish time to make music. That's the reason why the band's been successful all these years—that's all we ever did."

Although Gwen enjoys being married, she's no domestic goddess. "It's so embarrassing," she confessed in *Cosmo*. "I'm not very good at cleaning up and doing the homemaker thing. The one thing that makes me feel super-lucky about my financial success is that I have a housekeeper."

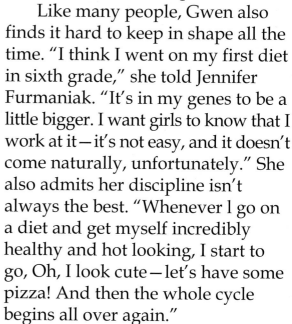

> Gwen also finds it hard to keep in shape all the time. "I think I went on my first diet in sixth grade."

Like many people, Gwen also finds it hard to keep in shape all the time. "I think I went on my first diet in sixth grade," she told Jennifer Furmaniak. "It's in my genes to be a little bigger. I want girls to know that I work at it—it's not easy, and it doesn't come naturally, unfortunately." She also admits her discipline isn't always the best. "Whenever l go on a diet and get myself incredibly healthy and hot looking, I start to go, Oh, I look cute—let's have some pizza! And then the whole cycle begins all over again."

Throughout 2003 and 2004, Gwen's album slowly came together. She found herself frequently terrified at the thought of working without Tony, Tom, and Adrian, and she often found herself crying out of anxiety. Still, she forced herself to keep going, telling the *Observer*, "Right now I'm all about trying things I've never done. I'm a woman and I'm 35. I don't have that much time left to do this kind of pop record. Let's be real."

Gwen also dabbled in acting, appearing as the 1930s movie sex symbol Jean Harlow in *The Aviator*, opposite Leonardo DiCaprio. How she got the part is pure

Hollywood—director Martin Scorsese saw a billboard featuring Gwen and decided she was perfect for the part.

"I was looking pretty fine and pretty blonde," Gwen laughingly told writer David Matthews, "and Martin [Scorsese] saw me beaming back at him. He sent me the script and I spent 15 minutes looking for Jean Harlow because it's such a small part. . . . I still had to audition, which was torturous. I wasn't used to that pressure, competing against other girls and full-on actresses, but I got through it."

She realized collaborating with the people on her album—such as OutKast's Andre 3000, Dr. Dre, and innovative producers The Neptunes—that she wants to learn how to play the guitar or piano, "so I don't have to rely on someone to collaborate with. I've written songs on guitar, but I don't play guitar good enough to be free. If I could play every chord? I could write a million songs."

For now, the ones she's writing are doing just fine. *Love, Angel, Music, Baby* was released in November 2004, and by the end of 2005 was certified triple platinum. More important for Stefani, at a concert in Fort Lauderdale on December 21, she announced she was pregnant.

According to wire service reports, Gwen told the audience, "This is the end of a huge chapter for me." She also acknowledged that she hadn't intended to go on tour

> *At a concert in Fort Lauderdale on December 21, 2005, Stefani announced she was pregnant.*

Happy parents-to-be Gwen and Gavin attend the 48th Annual Grammy Awards in February 2006 at the Staples Center in Los Angeles. Gwen officially announced her pregnancy at a December 2005 concert. Kingston James McGregor Rossdale was born May 26, 2006.

after finding out she was pregnant in October, but realized she needed "to sing my songs and have you sing them back to me one more time."

On May 26, 2006, Gwen gave birth to a healthy seven-and-a-half-pound boy at Los Angeles' Cedars-Sinai Medical Center. She and Gavin named their son Kingston James McGregor Rossdale.

Although Gwen has announced she'll take an indefinite break from performing to concentrate on motherhood, even prior to getting pregnant she seemed unsure what the future would hold.

"This is the first time in a long time that I don't know what's gonna happen next," she said in a 2005 *Observer* interview. "As a famous person you think how you're gonna end it [the celebrity life], get away and have a normal life. I imagine my children are going to save me from my vanity and be my passion and fill whatever fears I have of the amazing time I'm having right now being gone.

"I don't want to drop off and not be on the radio. . . . I don't want it to go away. But at the same time, I never expected to be here in the first place."

> Gwen has announced she'll take an indefinite break from performing to focus on motherhood.

CHRONOLOGY

1969   Gwendolyn Renée Stefani is born in Fullerton, California, on October 3
1972   Sister, Jill, is born
1974   Younger brother, Todd, is born
1986   Gwen agrees to sing backup in older brother Eric's new band
1987   Performs first professional gig in Long Beach, California; meets Tony Kanal; graduates from Loara High School
1988   Becomes No Doubt's new lead singer
1990   No Doubt records first demo tape
1991   No Doubt signs record deal with Interscope
1994   Eric leaves the band, then Tony breaks up with Gwen
2001   Gwen wins Grammy Award with Eve for Best Rap/Sung Collaboration ("Let Me Blow Ya Mind") in February
2002   No Doubt wins Grammy for "Hey Baby"; Gwen marries Gavin Rossdale September 17
2003   Gwen announces solo album; No Doubt wins Grammy for Best Pop Performance by a Group for "Underneath It All"
2004   *Love, Angel, Music, Baby* released; introduces LAMB clothing line; appears in *The Aviator*
2005   Works on *Hurricane Relief: Come Together Now,* which will aid victims of Hurricane Katrina; announces pregnancy; is nominated for 5 Grammys
2006   Gives birth to son Kingston James McGregor Rossdale on May 26

DISCOGRAPHY

2005   *Hurricane Relief: Come Together Now* (contributor, with other artists)
2004   *Love, Angel, Music, Baby* (solo); *Everything in Time*
2003   *Boom Box*
2001   *Rock Steady*
2000   *Return of Saturn*
1995   *Tragic Kingdom; Beacon Street Collection*
1992   *No Doubt*

FURTHER READING

Books

Hurst, Brandon. *Gwen Stefani.* London: Artnik, 2006.

Blankstein, Amy H. *The Story of Gwen Stefani.* London: Omnibus Press, 2006.

Works Consulted

Carlozo, Lou. "Just a Whirl. No Doubt, The Year Has Been Frenzied — But Gwen Took Time to Chat." *Chicago Tribune.* January 7, 1997.

Eliscu, Jenny. "I'll Cry Just Thinking About It." *The Observer.* January 30, 2005. http://observer.guardian.co.uk/magazine/story/0,11913,1400175,00.html

———— . "Gwen Cuts Loose." Rollingstone.com http://www.rollingstone.com/news/story/6822921/gwen_cuts_loose/

Furmaniak, Jennifer Kasle. "It's Good to Be Gwen Stefani." *Cosmopolitan.* June 6, 2004. http://magazines.ivillage.com/cosmopolitan/connect/chats/articles/0,,284422_634046,00.html

Griggs, Brandon. Tragic Kingdom fanzine. http://www.nodoubt.com/features/index.html

Hoggard, Liz. "Gwen Stefani: Blonde with extra bottle; Madonna thinks she is ripping her off, but who is the bigger star now?" *The Independent Sunday.* November 6, 2005.

Letkemann, Jessica. "No Doubt's Happy-Go-Lucky Ska-influenced Sound." *Circus,* February 1997. http://www.nodoubt.com/band/Articles/31Circus.htm

Matthews, David. "Film Interview: Hark the Herald Angel; How Rock Star Gwen Stefani Is Trying to Make It in Hollywood." *The Mirror.* December 24, 2004.

"No Doubt." VH-1, Behind the Music.

No Doubt International Fan Club. "John Spense." http://www.ndifc.com/bio/john.htm

Sexton, Paul. "Megastar? No Doubt About It." Scotsman.com. http://living.scotsman.com/music.cfm?id=1338212004

Wartofsky, Alona. "No Doubt's Gwen Stefani's happy sound delights millions of young fans." *Washington Post.* June 15, 1997.

Online

Gwen Stefani's official web site http://www.gwenstefani.com

No Doubt's web site http://www.nodoubt.com

INDEX